WHAT'S NEXT? WHAT'S NEXT?

?

THE FUTURE OF

Space Exploration

By Diane Bailey

W

FRANKLIN WATTS

LONDON • SYDNEY

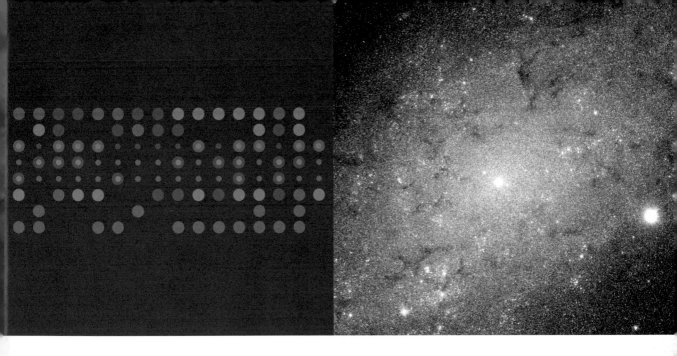

Contents

INTRODUCTION

For hundreds of miles in any direction, Mars is a deserted and seemingly dead planet. But imagine that in one place, there is life. Nestled beneath a rocky overhang are a cluster of climate-controlled domes. A colony of people live inside. Some came from Earth, but others were born here. Unlike the older colonists, the youngest have never seen a plant that wasn't growing indoors. They gaze in wonder at photos of oceans of water. They're surprised to learn that Earth's Moon crosses the sky only once a day. One day, their parents promise, they will go on holiday to Earth. But for now, they will have to strap on their oxygen packs and pressurised suits to go outside. Life on Mars isn't easy, but it is home.

No humans have actually set foot on Mars, but some countries are planning to visit Mars at some point in the future. The trip itself would take months using today's modes of transportation, and space travel is hard on the human body. Once they get there, the first astronauts will probably stay for several months. However, Mars doesn't have anything that's 'ready to use'. Humans can't breathe its atmosphere, it's very cold and there's no food. Scientists must develop machines that will let astronauts use Mars's resources to produce breathable air, water and fuel. They'll need to make sure that building materials will withstand freezing temperatures and different atmospheric conditions. Even with all the essentials, surviving in an alien environment will be both physically and mentally challenging. Humans have walked on the Moon, but Mars will require more creativity, better technology and a lot of hard work.

Mars, probably the next space stop for human visitors, has already been studied from afar (photo taken by the Hubble Space Telescope, left), and up-close (a Mars rover, above).

FROM THE GROUND UP

Space is only an eight-and-a-half-minute trip from Earth on board a space shuttle, but it has taken humans about 100,000 years to work out *how* to get there. A lot of time and preparation went into discovering how to cross the Kármán Line, the point 100 kilometres above the Earth that scientists identify as the 'start of space'.

Thousands of years ago, humans gazed up at the skies and wondered about the dots of light they saw. What were they? How far away were they? Why did some move? Many early Western astronomers believed that the planets, the Sun and other stars revolved around the Earth, but in 1543, Polish scientist Nicolaus Copernicus proposed a different idea. He argued that the Sun was the centre of this 'solar system'. Earth, he said, wasn't so special after all. His theory – which angered many people at the time but turned out to be correct – kicked off the modern age of astronomy.

In 1608, a Dutch lens maker called Hans Lippershey created a telescope. Telescopes were *the* technology to have in the 17th century as they brought the stars and planets into sharper focus. Italian scientist Galileo Galilei used one to identify four of Jupiter's moons. In 1609, the instrument helped Johannes Kepler, a German astronomer, develop a theory on how the planets moved. Over the next few centuries, more stars, planets and moons were discovered. By the 20th century, some scientists began to talk about actually visiting one of these heavenly bodies. But first, there was World War II (1939–45) to fight.

The contributions by
Galileo Galilei to astronomy
were vast. They included
improvements to the
telescope, the discovery
of Jupiter's moons and
observations of spots on
the Sun.

The idea of a rocket powered by liquid oxygen and hydrogen was not new when World War II began. A Russian scientist named Konstantin Tsiolkovsky had come up with that idea 35 years earlier. The United States, led by such physicists as Robert Goddard, built and launched rockets in the 1920s, and German scientists were working on them in the 1930s. However, the demand for missile weapons in World War II gave rocket science the boost it needed. By 1945, as the war was drawing to an end, the powerful V-2 rocket was developed and launched by Germany. It came too late to prevent Germany's defeat, but it laid the foundations for the technology that would take rockets into space.

After the war, relationships remained strained between countries that had been enemies or even allies. In particular, the United States and the Soviet Union had an uneasy truce that developed into decades of mistrust – a period of more than 40 years that would be known as the Cold War. Both countries possessed advanced weapons technology featuring rockets and nuclear warheads. Each wanted to demonstrate its technological might and superiority, but neither wanted an all-out war that could destroy the world. Instead, the rivals set their sights higher – much higher. The 'Space Race' had begun.

For about a decade, scientists in both countries worked to develop a rocket that could be launched into Earth's orbit – the elliptical path that an object takes when revolving around the planet.

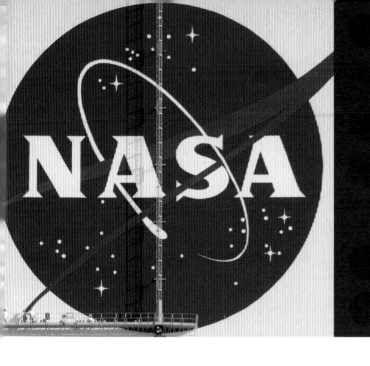

Konstantin Tsiolkovsky (opposite) laid much of the groundwork in the field of rocket science, and NASA capitalised on it two decades after the Russian's death in 1935.

The United States government was confident it would win the race, but on 4 October, 1957, it learned otherwise. On that day, the Soviet Union successfully launched *Sputnik 1*, an unmanned satellite that stayed in orbit for three months.

Although the United States had lost the race to be the first nation in space, it was determined to respond quickly. Two months after *Sputnik 1*, the Americans attempted to launch *Vanguard*. However, its rocket launcher only rose less that two metres off the launch pad before it lost power, crashed and exploded, prompting newspapers to call it 'Flopnik'. Finally, on 31 January, 1958, the United States successfully put a satellite, *Explorer 1*, into orbit, where it stayed for 12 years.

In the Soviet Union, the space programme was part of the armed forces. The United States, however, took a different approach. In 1958, it established an agency to focus on space exploration: the National Aeronautics and Space Administration (NASA). Wernher von Braun, a German-American scientist who worked for NASA, was convinced humans should travel in space. In 1958, he said, "Don't tell me that man doesn't belong out there. Man belongs wherever he wants to go, and he'll do plenty well when he gets there."

Both the United States and the Soviet Union were eager to build on their successes. Over the next few years, the Soviets kept scoring a series of firsts. In 1959, they sent a probe to the Moon. Then, in 1961, they reached another significant milestone. On the

Despite some tragedies, fatalities and setbacks, the Apollo programme was a success, placing a man on the Moon just eight years after President John F. Kennedy (right) declared government support for the programme.

Vostok 1 mission, Soviet cosmonaut (the Russian term for astronaut) Yuri Gagarin became the first human to enter space on a trip that lasted 108 minutes. In 1965, a Soviet cosmonaut performed the first extra-vehicular activity (EVA), or spacewalk, leaving the safety of the spacecraft with only a tether to connect him. In 1966, the Soviets sent a probe to another planet, Venus.

However, there was still another big first to come, and this honour would be claimed by the United States. Challenged in 1961 by US president John F. Kennedy to put a man on the Moon, NASA began the Apollo programme. On 20 July, 1969, astronauts Neil Armstrong and Buzz Aldrin became the first humans to walk on the Moon. In all, twelve astronauts had walked on the Moon by the end of the Apollo programme. Going to the Moon was an impressive technical achievement and a huge source of pride for the United States. Now it was time to take even bigger steps.

NASA officials decided to explore deeper into the solar system. In the late 1970s, the outer planets – from Jupiter to Neptune – came into alignment. NASA scientists wanted to propel a spacecraft along this path by using Jupiter's powerful gravity as a type of slingshot, which would make the craft travel more quickly and require less fuel. Sadly, this idea of a 'Grand Tour' of the planets didn't happen as planned. However, in 1972 and 1973, the unmanned probes *Pioneer 10* and *Pioneer 11* left Earth, followed by the twin spacecraft *Voyager 1* and *Voyager 2* in 1977. Between them, they would fly past and photograph Jupiter, Saturn, Uranus and Neptune and use radio signals to send back scientific data about these four 'gas giants'.

Despite our fascination with these outer planets, a much closer planet holds even more interest for both scientists and the general public. The exploration of Mars has dominated both science fiction and science fact for decades, but it has proved difficult. It took five years of failed missions before a successful flyby was achieved in 1965 by the US spacecraft *Mariner 4*. The Soviet Union attempted several times to send probes to Mars in the early 1970s, but

VAN ALLEN UNCOVERS A THREAT

James Van Allen was less interested in putting something into space than he was in getting something out of it: data. An astrophysicist from Iowa, USA, Van Allen was convinced something far above Earth's atmosphere was producing radiation. When the United States launched its Explorer 1 satellite in 1958, Van Allen made sure that a Geiger counter (a device that measures radiation) was on board. The data it collected confirmed the existence of rings – or belts – of radiation around Earth. Because radiation can damage scientific instruments, identifying the Van Allen radiation belts was important, prompting engineers to design spacecraft that would protect instruments and later, people.

James Van Allen worked as a navy officer and rocket scientist during World War II. He then went on to teach physics at the University of Iowa from 1951 to 1985.

In space exploration, it is common for costly spacecraft such as *Galileo* (right) never to return to Earth. Sadly, sometimes the cost is in human lives, such as the *Challenger* crew (below).

COSMIC GERMS

The orbiting spacecraft, Galileo, sent to study Jupiter in 1989, was not sterilised before it left Earth. So when it discovered possible evidence of an underground ocean on Europa (one of Jupiter's moons), scientists had to make a tough call. The possibility of water meant the possibility of life, and Earthly germs could be deadly to foreign forms of life. NASA has rules to protect other moons or planets from being contaminated, so before they lost control of Galileo, which was running out of fuel, mission commanders sent it to burn up in Jupiter's atmosphere rather than risk it crashing into Europa.

although some of them landed, they were not able to send back any data. Finally, in 1976, the United States succeeded with its *Viking* spacecraft. There were more Mars missions throughout the 1980s and 1990s. However, time and again, scientists' hope for a mission would be followed by a dismal failure. So many Mars missions failed that scientists joked about a 'galactic ghoul' that ate the probes!

There were also more tragic setbacks. The US space shuttle programme, which began in 1972, built reusable spacecraft that could transport astronauts and cargo to space stations. While most shuttle missions succeeded, there were two major disasters. In 1986, *Challenger* exploded shortly after launch. Then, in 2003, *Columbia* disintegrated as it re-entered Earth's atmosphere. In each incident, all of the crew lost their lives. The programme came to an end in 2011, due to safety concerns over the ageing spacecraft.

In the years to come, astronauts will use smaller, newly designed vehicles to travel to the International Space Station (ISS), where scientists conduct research in low Earth orbit. The Soviets were again leaders in the creation of space stations, paving the way for more to come when it put the first station, *Salyut*, into orbit in 1971. The United States followed with *Skylab* in 1973, and then the Soviets launched *Mir* in 1986. Construction began on the ISS in 1998, and today, 16 different countries have contributed to it. Having so far cost more than £65 billion (US$100 billion), it is estimated to be the most expensive object ever built.

NEW PRIORITIES

People have long been motivated by the reward of simply being able to do something – and of doing it first. But space exploration is too expensive to be undertaken simply as a hobby or a source of pride. People and machines that go into space need to be able to do something important once they get there. The trick is in deciding what that 'something' is. Today, space programmes around the world are working on better technologies for travel and exploration. But first they have to answer a basic question: Why go?

It's been a while since humans have been anywhere further than the ISS. Manned missions to the Moon stopped in the 1970s, and public interest in space exploration largely fell off in the last part of the 20th century. The Moon had been seen as the ultimate destination in the 1960s, but 10 years later, many regarded it with a 'been there, done that' attitude. Current technology couldn't take humans any further, and so the focus turned to robotic missions.

From a scientific point of view, we are exploring space to gather data in order to better understand our universe. Including how the Earth and the solar system were formed, to learn about other planets, stars and galaxies, and to look for other forms of life. Humans need to understand this data, but they don't have to be there to collect it. Robots, built to contend with extreme temperatures and poisonous gases, can collect samples from other planets that humans can't yet travel to. And if a robot is lost or destroyed on a mission, it's an expensive disappointment but not a tragedy.

The risk to humans in space exploration would greatly increase if we explored further than the Moon (left). Spacewalks (above) are one of the most dangerous tasks.

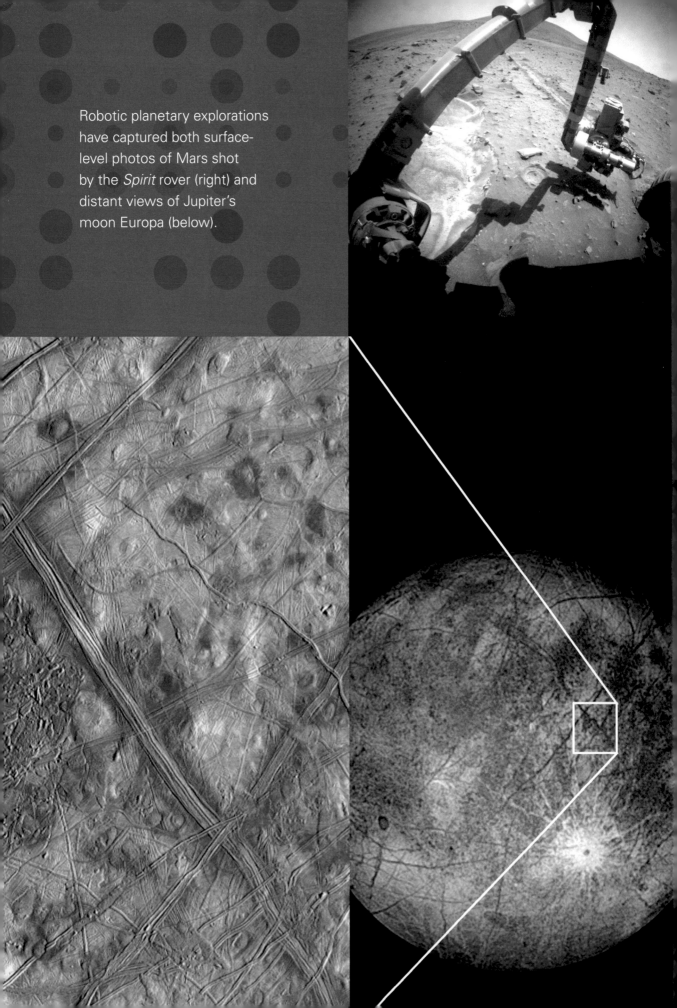

Robotic planetary explorations have captured both surface-level photos of Mars shot by the *Spirit* rover (right) and distant views of Jupiter's moon Europa (below).

In 2004, two US rovers – named *Spirit* and *Opportunity* – landed
on Mars. Their missions were supposed to last only a few months,
but these plucky little rovers lived up to their names. Despite getting
stuck in the soil and enduring violent dust storms, they sent valuable
data back to Earth for years. *Spirit* fell silent in 2010, but *Opportunity*
was still going strong in 2013.

In 2008, the spacecraft *Phoenix* confirmed there was water
in the Martian soil. Water means the possibility of life, fuelling
speculation about the single biggest question in space exploration:
Are humans the only intelligent form of life in the Universe?

That simple (and so far unanswerable) question has served as
the basis for countless science-fiction books and films. It's also a
fundamental issue for scientists. Astrobiology is the study of life in
space. Understanding the origin of life on Earth, and looking for life
off Earth, drives much of space exploration. Scientists aren't looking
for little green men on Mars, of course. If there were any, surely a
space probe would have taken a picture of them by now. Instead,
they are looking for *evidence* that life once existed in a place other
than Earth – or that it could exist in the future.

Research on Mars, for example, shows that the planet may
once have been warmer. One of Jupiter's moons, Europa, is also a
good candidate for containing life. Although the surface is frozen,
there appear to be warmer spots underground, suggesting it could
be similar to the conditions under which life started on Earth.
Scientists are also searching other solar systems for signs of life. In

While decades of space travel have given astronauts experience with weightlessness, more remains to be learned about how plants grow in zero-gravity environments.

'Yecora Rojo'
83 days old

2010, American astronomers announced they had found the planet Gliese 581g. The planet itself is outside our own solar system and too far away to see with a telescope, but the researchers had studied the movements of other, nearby objects for 11 years and concluded they were being caused by the gravitational pull of a planetary body. With this data, the researchers deduced that Gliese 581g was located in the 'habitable zone' of its parent star, meaning it was in a place that could make its climate neither too hot nor too cold. This 'Goldilocks planet' – about 20 light years from Earth – could be just right for life. Early in 2011, other researchers said they could not find the planet again, but it still might be there. Just the possibility was enough to excite many scientists.

In addition to looking for other forms of life, scientists are working on ways to make space more habitable for earthly creatures. On the ISS, experiments show how plants and other substances can grow in a weightless environment. Researchers can

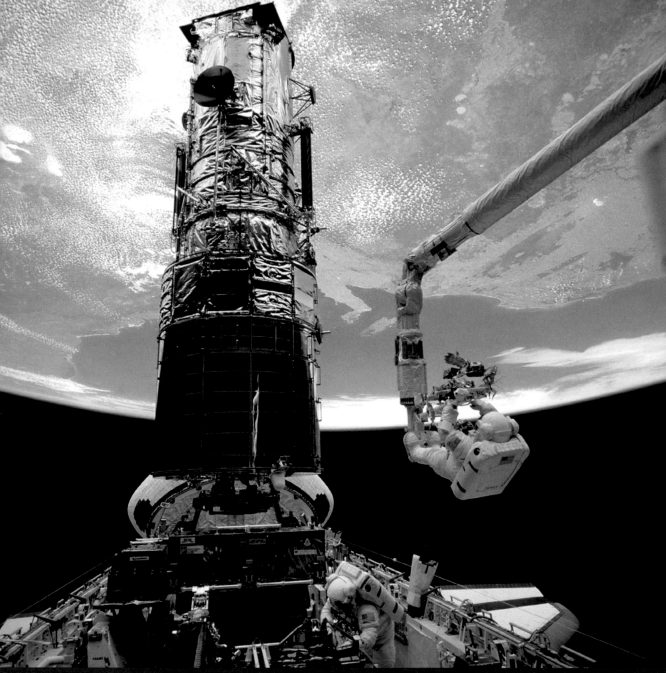

A LONG, WONDERFUL LOOK

Since 1990, as scientists have been discussing the means and merits of sending astronauts to the Moon and Mars, the Hubble Space Telescope has been gazing into the distant realms of space. This powerful, 10.9 tonne observatory, named after American astronomer Edwin Hubble, orbits Earth at an altitude of 595 kilometres, capturing stunning photographs of stars, planetary systems and other cosmic bodies. In January 2011, Hubble detected the most distant object ever seen in the universe: a galaxy estimated to be 13.2 billion light years away. "After 20 years of opening our eyes to the universe around us," said NASA astrophysicist Jon Morse, "Hubble continues to awe and surprise astronomers."

Since its mirror was repaired in 1993 (opposite), the Hubble Space Telescope has captured countless stunning images like this distant nebula, or gas cloud (left).

see how certain metals or other materials respond, to determine if they can be used for building things in space. They even experiment on themselves. Astronauts who spend months on the ISS don't feel the pull of gravity. Without gravity to work against, their fitness levels decline and their muscles and bone mass deteriorate. Astronauts now have health plans to make sure they get plenty of exercise in space, using specially adapted treadmills and stationary bicycles, to combat the effects of weightlessness.

One unique thing about the ISS, or other satellites placed in orbit, is that they have a dazzling view of planet Earth. Pictures taken from the ISS have produced some of the most accurate topographical and environmental data that scientists currently have. Countries such as India, Iran, Brazil and South Korea all have space programmes they hope will help solve some of their problems by locating natural resources and improving communication links through satellites.

Space exploration increasingly involves international collaboration (right, a multinational space shuttle crew) and private efforts (below, Richard Branson on left and on right, Burt Rutan).

While the Space Race of the 1960s certainly had a scientific basis, it developed from the rivalry between the United States and the Soviet Union. Political competition, even more than science, was the 'fuel' that inspired people in this era to go into space. For more than 40 years, space was exclusive. Only two nations – the United States and the Soviet Union (later Russia) – knew how to send people into space. In 2003, China joined that club when it successfully sent a taikonaut into orbit. In 2010, China announced it plans to send people to the Moon by 2025.

Today, cooperation is valued more than competition in space exploration. Even a single mission can cost billions, so some countries are deciding that two bank accounts are better than one. And sometimes, even space programmes need a little help from their friends (and former enemies). After the US space shuttle *Columbia* disintegrated on re-entry into the Earth's atmosphere

RUTAN'S PRIZE WINNER

The Ansari X challenge was big: build a manned, reusable spacecraft and send it into space. Then bring it back. Then do it again. All in two weeks. The prize was pretty big, too: £6.6 million (US$10 million). In 2004, American aerospace engineer Burt Rutan won the prize with his design, called SpaceShipOne. Since then, the space travel company Virgin Galactic plans to offer spaceflights using another of his designs, SpaceShipTwo. Hundreds of bookings have already been taken, but the craft will need to undergo further testing before the public are allowed onboard. Rutan thinks space should be open to the public, and he wants to build a lot of ships to take them there. "I'm getting a commercial system going for one reason," he said. "I don't think anybody else will."

in 2003, NASA temporarily grounded its remaining fleet of three space shuttles. Russia was the only other country with operating shuttles, so for two years, US astronauts had to hitch a lift with the Russian cosmonauts.

Whatever lofty goals scientists have for exploration, the first thing they have to address is the practical matter of transportation. Rocket fuel is expensive, and it takes a lot of it to launch heavy vehicles out of Earth's gravity. It costs roughly $10,000 per 1 lb (equivalent to about £6,425 per 454 grams) to send something into space. That's almost £1 million (US$1.5 million) for each astronaut and another £82 (US$125) for every pen they bring with them! Even though rockets travel at thousands of kilometres per hour, that's still slow in cosmic terms. This limits how far into space we can go. Another issue limiting exploratory efforts is the fact that, as soon as humans board a spacecraft, the primary concern is not science but the safety of the crew. This means that if difficult decisions must be made about taking risks, missions will usually err on the side of caution when human lives are involved.

NASA's recently retired space shuttles had nowhere near enough speed or range to approach deep-space objects such as supernovas, or exploding stars (opposite).

FURTHER AND FASTER

One thing about robots is that they don't argue about who will sit by the window. Nor do they complain about feeling hungry or tired. Because most space exploration is about conducting hard scientific research, some experts think humans should stay at home and send machines to do the hard work. Alien environments may be too hostile for humans, even those wearing protective spacesuits, and people are limited by the length of time they can travel because they have to take all their food and supplies with them. And of course, they might also get homesick!

Robots may be able to do even more in the future. Better computer parts will let them perform more accurate calculations to analyse the data they collect. They may even use this data to 'decide' on their own what should be explored in depth. Meanwhile, advances in mechanics will improve how they bend, pick up objects, or navigate over rough terrain. Robots are able to go to the same places a human can, as well as where a human *can't* go. They could also act as helpful companions to human astronauts. In 2012, *Robonaut 2* was taken on board the ISS to test how well it could work with human astronauts. With its humanoid design – it even has hands – it has already performed some tasks for the astronauts, and more ambitious projects are planned for the future.

But some people think it's time for humans to return to space. In 2010, US president Barack Obama directed NASA to focus on sending manned missions to an asteroid in about 2025, and then on to Mars in the 2030s. Although exploring space can help explain

NASA has built four *Robonaut* models for testing; the space agency hopes to perfect the robots for future missions. One Robonaut – Robonaut 2 – has already been tried out on the ISS.

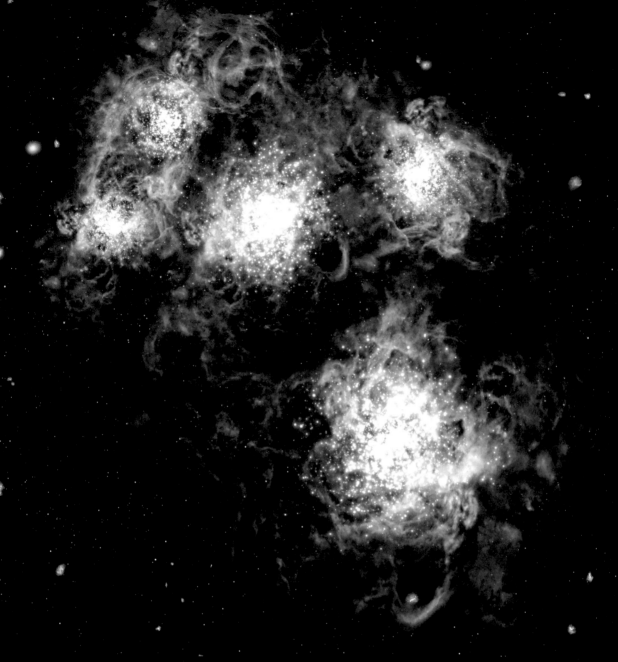

STARS IN THEIR EYES

Digging for gold on an asteroid? Growing plants on Mars? It could happen.
Some scientists are planning ahead to a day when life on Earth becomes impossible
because of natural or man-made disasters, or the exhaustion of resources. They
are studying other planets and moons so people could move there if necessary.
Researchers are excited about the possibilities of space, and a lot of today's
exploration is driven by economic and social concerns. However, the biggest driving
force is still curiosity. What's out there? That basic desire to find out is the most
human motivation of all.

and improve life on Earth, some discoveries may also help people to survive *off* Earth. "Life on Earth is at the ever-increasing risk of being wiped out by a disaster," said British astrophysicist Stephen Hawking. "It is important for the human race to spread out into space for the survival of the species." If that happens, the Moon or Mars will probably be the first stop.

Because the Moon is relatively close, at about 380,000 kilometres away from Earth and because humans have some experience there, it's a logical starting point. However, a Moon base might not be *on* the Moon – it could be *in* it. Just as underground burrows shelter animals in winter, an in-ground settlement would protect people from the Moon's extreme temperatures, which range from -233°C at night to 123°C in the daytime. It would also shield them from radiation and help prevent air loss. On the surface of the Moon, astronauts would constantly be disturbing Moon dust, which tends to clog up the joints of spacesuits. To solve this problem, astronauts might heat the dust to high temperatures, melting it into hard glass to create sturdy, dust-free pathways.

A Martian colony might also be underground, but it could be built on the surface, too. The atmosphere on Mars protects it from extreme temperature variations, but it's still pretty cold – on average it is about -63°C. To let in sunlight and hold in warmth, a colony on Mars might be housed within a series of glass domes. Food would be grown inside. At least at first, the diet would probably be exclusively vegetarian. It would be like a large terrarium, where the chemicals needed by humans and plants would balance each other out. When astronauts went outside, they might drive around in sturdy six-wheeled vehicles that could move forwards, backwards and sideways. Planes, specially designed to fly in the thin atmosphere and reduced gravity of Mars, could be developed to explore the planet from above its difficult, rocky terrain.

The success of outposts or colonies will depend on the use of local resources. On the Moon, for example, scientists could extract oxygen from the soil. Oxygen is the main ingredient in rocket fuel, and fuel takes up the most space and weight on a spacecraft.

The illustration to the right depicts an artist's vision of what Mars – its land terraformed and atmosphere modified – might look like one day far in the future.

If astronauts could make their own fuel once they got to the Moon, then they could bring more supplies or equipment for a longer trip. In addition, they could produce and store fuel on the Moon to use for future missions. On Mars, the abundant carbon dioxide found in the Martian atmosphere could be converted into methane, which could also be used as fuel.

Eventually, human colonists might turn to terraforming, the process of changing a landscape or environment to make it more like Earth. Theoretically, humans could use machines to produce large amounts of greenhouse gases, which store heat, to warm up the atmosphere. These gases can be produced from the elements already on Mars. Colonisation is still at least a couple of decades in the future, and terraforming would take a century or more once it begins. But many scientists believe it will happen. According to Christopher McKay, a planetary scientist with NASA's Ames Research Center, "Space colonisation will be the ultimate camping trip. It'll test our equipment, it'll test our planning, it'll test us. But it'll be worth it."

The tricky problem of transportation remains, however. NASA's New Horizons spacecraft left for Pluto in 2006. Even travelling at the fastest launch speed ever for a man-made object, it won't get there until 2015. If spacecraft could go at the speed of light, that would be handy indeed. One solution is a solar sail – perhaps as big as hundreds of kilometres wide – made out of micro-thin fibres. These sails would

PICK A PLACE

Should the Moon be a destination, a pit stop on the way to more distant places, or an option skipped altogether? The Moon is much closer than Mars and could serve as a training ground for more ambitious manned missions or colonisation efforts in the future. However, it may not have as much scientific or economic potential. American Marc Cohen is a space architect, someone who specialises in designing and building structures for space environments. He says, "Aside from being the largest local piece of barren rock on which to land a spacecraft, [the Moon] is virtually devoid of resources." For this reason, many scientists favour going directly to Mars.

be attached to a spacecraft and powered by light (from the Sun or lasers), which would create propulsion. Solar-sail spacecraft would be able to travel at roughly 1/10th the speed of light, or at about 28,800 kilometres per second. In 2010, the Japan Aerospace Exploration Agency launched *Ikaros*, a spacecraft powered in part by a solar sail, bound for Venus. As this technology improves, Japan hopes to use it to send a mission to Jupiter by about 2020. Another option for space fuel is hydrogen fusion. Spacecraft using this type of power would get much better mileage than existing spacecraft, and, because hydrogen is readily available in the atmosphere of many planets, there would be gas stations conveniently located along the way!

Faster and more fuel-efficient modes of travel mean that spacecraft can go further. A journey to Proxima Centauri, the closest star other than our Sun, could take about 60 years instead of the 165,000 it would take today's space shuttle. Of course, not all trips are long ones. In the future, astronauts taking short hops to the ISS might use a 'space elevator', a 96,000-kilometre long cable. This could be anchored to Earth at the top of a tall tower or mountain, or in a mobile location such as a ship, which would enable the cable to be moved to avoid storms or space junk. Such an elevator could be ready as soon as the 2020s.

Solar-sail spacecraft are already in use (Japanese researcher Yuichi Tsuda explains the design, opposite). But futuristic 'space hotel' modules (left) are still Earth-bound.

While NASA and other national space agencies developed the technology to get humans into space, private businesses are now building their own spacecraft and booking space flights. A handful of private companies around the world are working on developing spacecraft that are cheaper to operate and available for private use. Entrepreneur, Sir Richard Branson, is planning to offer trips into space aboard his SpaceShipTwo spacecraft for £128,000 (US$200,000) for a two-hour flight. Once people get into space, of course, they may need somewhere to stay. American businessman Robert Bigelow runs an aerospace research company, Bigelow Aerospace, that has developed marshmallow-shaped modules that people could inhabit in space. In 2006, the company launched prototypes of the modules into space, and NASA has bought one for the ISS. Companies or governments could rent out these modules for research, or they could even act as hotels for tourists. They may not have big beds or room service, but the view will be fantastic!

MAKING THE LEAP

There is probably a long wait ahead before there are traffic lights on the Moon, cable TV on Mars or vending machines in a floating, space hotel. Setting up shop in space is going to take a lot of planning, and the first hurdle is working out where to go.

Earth's closest planets are Venus and Mars. Venus is far too hot (about 452°C) and inhospitable for humans. That leaves Mars. Mars is cold, and the atmosphere isn't breathable, but at least it won't burn up people or machines. The problem is, even at its closest point Mars is 55 million km away. It would at least take a six-month trip from Earth to reach the planet. (And travelling 'out of season'; when Mars's orbit is out of sync with Earth's, makes the journey even longer.) If people are going to visit Mars, it makes sense to settle in for a little while once they get there.

The Moon, on the other hand, is more like a weekend away. It has less gravity than Mars and no atmosphere at all, but it's much closer. If anything happens to astronauts while they're on the Moon, there's a possibility that people on Earth could rescue them. But if anything goes wrong on Mars, the crew is on its own. As University of Tennessee scientist Lawrence Taylor says, "There's going to be a hazard, and if we think it's dangerous to go to the Moon, what about Mars? You just can't bail out and go home." Even seeking advice would be difficult. When *Apollo 13* suffered a power loss on its way to the Moon in 1970, the command centre in Houston, Texas, knew about the problem within seconds. But the communications delay from Mars is more than half an hour.

Setting up bases or colonies on Mars (above) or the Moon (left) will be a difficult task, as both of them feature barren, rocky landscapes with few ready-to-use resources.

GOING GREEN?

It's red against green in the Mars Trilogy, a series of books written in the 1990s by American author Kim Stanley Robinson. The year is 2026, and people have moved to Mars. One group, the 'Greens', want to change Mars to make it more habitable. The 'Reds' think they should leave it alone. Three books (Red Mars, Green Mars and Blue Mars) trace the terraforming of Mars over two centuries as plants and liquid water are introduced into the environment and allow people to live there. Although some aspects of terraforming are technically possible, it's currently too expensive and would probably generate a lot of controversy.

Also, researchers still don't know how humans will respond to living in space for more than a few weeks at a time. A Mars mission, including travel time, will take almost two years. Humans start to show physical effects from spending time in space after only a few weeks. Muscles break down, bone density decreases and the immune system gets weaker. Sleep patterns are disrupted because they are tied to Earth's cycles of light and dark. Finding ways to combat these will be necessary for extended space travel.

Another issue is how crew members will interact with each other, and how they will respond to being away from family and friends for so long. It's expensive to send too many people, but too few could be disastrous. If an astronaut gets hurt – or worse – on the trip, the crew will need someone who can take over his or her job. Chris Lewicki, a former flight engineer with NASA, says, "In space, we know how to 'boldly go' at this point, but we have very poor demonstrated experience in staying there."

Experiments on the ISS may help bring in some necessary data. There, scientists can study the effects of weightlessness on people and plants. Meanwhile, research in biotechnology could prove useful to humans once they reach a destination. For example, scientists could develop synthetic, or man-made, life forms that help transform an environment or that could be used as food for livestock brought to support colonists.

WINNER OF THE
NEBULA AWARD FOR BEST NOVEL

RED
MARS

"A STAGGERING BOOK.
THE BEST NOVEL ON
THE COLONIZATION OF
MARS THAT HAS EVER
BEEN WRITTEN.
IT SHOULD BE REQUIRED
READING FOR THE COLONISTS
OF THE NEXT CENTURY."
—Arthur C. Clarke

KIM STANLEY
ROBINSON
BESTSELLING AUTHOR OF BLUE MARS

WINNER OF THE
HUGO AWARD FOR BEST NOVEL

GREEN
MARS

"ROBINSON'S IS ONE
OF THE MOST
IMPRESSIVE BODIES OF
WORK IN MODERN
SCIENCE FICTION."
—The New York Times
Book Review

KIM STANLEY
ROBINSON
BESTSELLING AUTHOR OF BLUE MARS

WINNER OF THE
HUGO AWARD FOR BEST NOVEL

BLUE
MARS

"A LANDMARK
IN THE HISTORY
OF THE GENRE."
—The New York
Times Book Review

KIM STANLEY
ROBINSON
HUGO AND NEBULA AWARD-WINNING
AUTHOR OF GREEN MARS

The human body seems
ill-equipped for extended
space exploration, as a
lack of gravity quickly
leads to a deterioration in
strength in both muscle
fibres and bones.

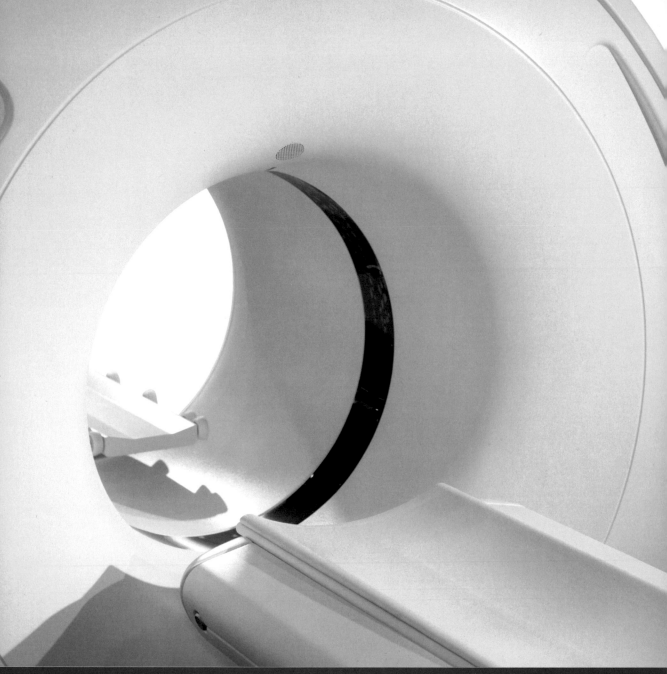

NOW AVAILABLE IN STORES

Technology developed by NASA doesn't stop in space. It's used today in all kinds of items and machines on Earth, including smoke detectors, wireless headphones and transparent braces. The technology used in CAT scans – computerised X-rays that combine several images – came from scientists enhancing pictures taken of the Moon. Athletic shoes have shock-absorbing materials that were first used in Moon boots. Sunglasses that block ultraviolet light rays, which can damage people's eyes, developed from research into ways of shielding astronauts from harsh sunlight. And since there aren't any electrical sockets on the Moon, we can thank space technology for cordless power tools as well.

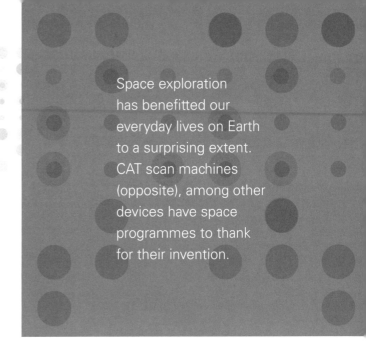

Space exploration has benefitted our everyday lives on Earth to a surprising extent. CAT scan machines (opposite), among other devices have space programmes to thank for their invention.

The single biggest problem with future space exploration will be getting people – or robots – where they need to go. Distances are mind-bogglingly vast. Even within our own solar system (and there are potentially billions more), journeys are months or years long, and few people want to be stuck on a spaceship that long. With current technologies, only the Moon and Mars are within reach of human travellers. If people are really going to journey across the final frontier, they're going to need better spacecraft.

To improve space travel, advances in nanotechnology, the science involving the creation and manipulation of extremely tiny objects, could help build spaceships that are lighter and require less fuel. Ships could also be made stronger and better able to handle the dangers in space, such as collisions with space junk or bursts of radiation. On the ISS, devices measure the atmosphere to find out how it affects the travel of spacecraft, with the aim of making it safer and faster. Some instruments study the ionosphere, which affects communications signals. This information will help keep astronauts in touch with Earth.

Robotic space travel has its own hurdles. In their 2008 book *Robots in Space*, authors Roger Launius and Howard McCurdy write, "The ideal space travellers would be as hardy as bacteria and as smart as computer geeks." Unfortunately, bacteria tend to be a bit dull, and human geeks occasionally get ill. Only machines can be healthy and smart all the time, but that will still require good engineering. Space-ready robots will have to be resistant to extreme

temperature changes and radiation. They will need reliable energy sources. They'll need to be strong, flexible, and pre-programmed with enough intelligence to get themselves out of difficult situations (if necessary). Robots can do a lot already, but to go further and do more, advances in materials and computing power will be vital.

Even if people could live in space, many would want to stay closer to home. But everyone needs a holiday once in a while, and space tourism is a growing business. The desire for quick trips, by ordinary people, may provide the incentive for developing new, lower-cost technologies. In 2004, American aerospace engineer Burt Rutan won the Ansari X Prize, which awarded £6.6 million (US$10 million) for the development of a manned, reusable spacecraft. Currently, the Internet company Google is sponsoring the Lunar X Prize, offering an award to the team that can land a robot on the Moon, which can then travel at least 500 metres and send pictures and other data back to Earth.

Contests such as these have helped encourage private development, and now government agencies can reap the benefits as well. In 2010, NASA offered to buy data and technologies from several teams competing for the Lunar X Prize. The merger of public agencies and private companies could greatly help space exploration, especially if responsibilities were divided up. For example, future flights to the ISS might be handled by private companies. Then, government agencies such as NASA could devote their full attention to the bigger – and more difficult – jobs of further exploring the Moon, Mars or asteroids.

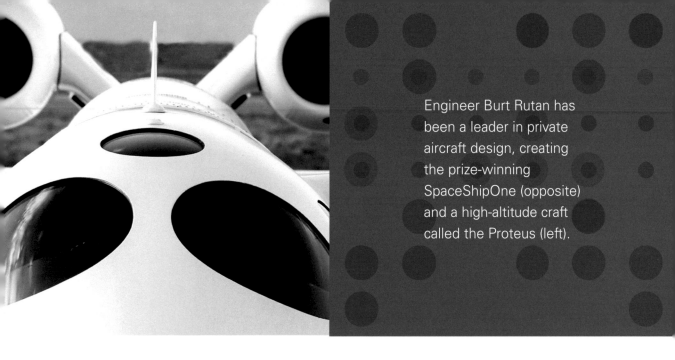

Engineer Burt Rutan has been a leader in private aircraft design, creating the prize-winning SpaceShipOne (opposite) and a high-altitude craft called the Proteus (left).

International cooperation will also speed up the pace of future space exploration, although political mistrust may hold things back. "I don't think any major effort in space will again be done by a single nation," said Tom Henricks, a former NASA astronaut. "They may each have individual sub goals, but it's a human endeavour to go to Mars, and I think that's the way it needs to be approached."

Curiosity. That's one reason people explore space, so it's an apt name for the Mars Science Laboratory rover that landed on Mars in August 2012. Of course, not everyone is in agreement about *why* to go into space, or *where* to go, or even *who* should go. Answering those questions is the first step in any new undertaking. Then comes the hard work – taking ideas from the drawing board and putting them into deep space. But exploring space is like solving a mystery. With each new clue that's discovered, scientists are eager to find more. The universe is vast, but it's within reach – one small step at a time.

GLOSSARY

alignment in space, when planets appear to line up

allies nations working together, particularly during a war

astrophysicist a scientist who studies the movements and properties of planets, stars and other celestial bodies

colony a group of people who leave their native country and settle in a new land, but remain closely associated with or controlled by their homeland

commercial relating to the buying and selling of goods and services

cosmonaut an astronaut from Russia (or the former Soviet Union)

elliptical in space, the circular or oval path an object takes when orbiting another (usually larger) object

gas giants Jupiter, Saturn, Uranus and Neptune – the four large planets mostly made up of gases

Goldilocks planet a planet that falls within the habitable zone of our solar system, where temperatures are neither too hot nor too cold

humanoid a machine that is designed to resemble humans and exhibit human-like behaviour

hydrogen a colourless, highly flammable gas; the most abundant element in the Universe

hydrogen fusion a nuclear reaction that forcefully combines, or 'glues', hydrogen atoms together and in the process releases a tremendous amount of energy

incentive a reason to do something

ionosphere the upper region of the Earth's (and some other planet's) atmosphere that contains electrons and electrically charged atoms and molecules.

light year a measurement of the distance light can travel in one year; nearly 10 million million kilometres

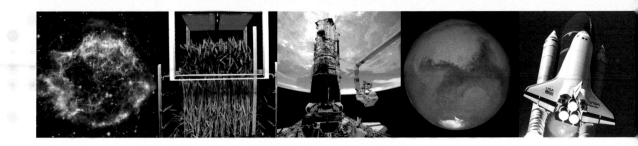

modules self-contained units. Often part of a set or larger structure

navigate to establish a proper course of travel or action

nuclear warheads explosive charges attached to missiles or bombs that explode with the enormous power of nuclear energy, which is energy produced by the splitting or fusing of atoms, the smallest particles that make up an object

probe an unmanned, robotic spacecraft that is sent to explore space or another celestial body

propel to use force or energy to make something move forwards

prototypes the first designs or models of a new technology or manufacturing process

radiation the process of sending out energy in the form of waves or particles; in excessive amounts, it can harm or kill living organisms

rovers robotic spacecraft designed to travel on the surface of another moon or planet

satellite an object placed into Earth's orbit to receive and transmit information over long distances

space junk the collection of man-made objects, such as spacecraft fragments and discarded equipment, that float through space; it is also called space debris

taikonaut an astronaut from China

terraforming the process of transforming the landscape of a planet so that it resembles Earth

terrarium a contained environment that can sustain itself without outside interference

topographical describing the physical aspects of a landscape, such as size, shape and features

FURTHER READING

Space Travel Guides (series) by Giles Sparrow (Franklin Watts, 2013)
Wonders of the Universe by Prof. Brian Cox and Andrew Cohen
  (Collins, 2011)
The Earth and Space (series) by Steve Parker (Wayland, 2009)
The World in Infographics: Space by Jon Richards and Ed Simkins
  (Wayland, 2012)
Eye on the Universe: The Incredible Hubble Space Telescope
  (American Space Missions, Astronauts, Exploration and Discovery)
  by Michael D. Cole (Enslow Publishers, 2013)
Inventors and Innovators: Pioneers in Astronomy and Space
  Exploration by Michael Anderson (Rosen, 2012)

WEBSITES

NASA

http://www.nasa.gov/

The official website of America's space agency is packed with information on all aspects of space exploration and includes sections specifically for younger readers.

National Space Society

http://www.nss.org/

This site is devoted to the possibilities of future space travel and especially outer space settlements, with sections discussing potential colonies on the Moon and Mars.

INDEX

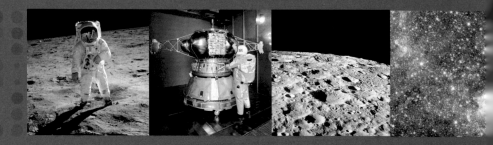

First published in the UK in 2013 by

Franklin Watts
338 Euston Road
London NW1 3BH

First published by Creative Education
P.O. Box 227, Mankato, Minnesota 56002
Creative Education is an imprint of The Creative Company
www.thecreativecompany.us
Copyright © 2013 Creative Education
International copyright reserved in all countries. No part of this book may be
reproduced in any form without written permission from the publisher.

ISBN: 978 1 4451 2378 3
Dewey number: 629.4'1

A CIP catalogue record for this book is available from the British Library.

Printed in China

Franklin Watts is a division of Hachette Children's Books,
 an Hachette Uk Company
www.hachette.co.uk

Design and production by The Design Lab
Art direction by Rita Marshall

Photographs by Alamy (Everett Collection Inc., RIA Novosti), Corbis (Armando
Arorizo/ZUMA, Jim Sugar/Science Faction, William James Warren), Dreamstime
(Pavel Losevsky, Peterfactors), Getty Images (Buyenlarge, John B. Carnett/Bonnier
Corporation, NASA/ESA, Spencer Platt, Stocktrek Images, Ted Thai/Time Life Pictures,
Time Life Pictures/NASA, Yoshikazu Tsuno/AFP), iStockphoto (Steven Wynn), NASA
(G. Bacon, ESA, Goddard Space Flight Center, Jim Grossmann, The Hubble Heritage
Team, James B. Irwin, JPL/Caltech, JPL/University of Arizona, Space Telescope
Science Institute/Rochester Institute of Technology)

Cover: An astronaut on an International Space Station spacewalk
Page 1: Astronaut Buzz Aldrin on the moon in 1969
Page 2: Construction work on the International Space Station